Dress Me Like a Prizefighter

Poems by Catherine Strayhall

Spartan
Press

Spartan Press

Kansas City, Missouri

spartanpresskc.com

Spartan
Press

Copyright © Catherine Strayhall, 2024

First Edition: 1 3 5 7 9 10 8 6 4 2

ISBN: 978-1-958182-53-6

LCCN: 2023951372

Author photo: Catherine Strayhall

Acknowledgments

Thank you to the following editors, journals, and organizations that first hosted versions of these poems:

Johnson County Arts & Heritage Center: "Wayfarer Memory," "hold fast and run like hell," "Aubade to Kansas City"

elementia: "kawaakari"

The Kansas State Collegian: "The Air Was Heavy and the Days Were Long"

Poets Reading the News: "to the yellow cardinal of alabaster, alabama," "I Leave Monet's *Water Lilies* at Every Shooting," "my battery is low," "love notes and dissent"

Thank you...

To Spartan Press and Jason Ryberg, for giving this manuscript a home. There's no place like Kansas City.

To my parents, for taking my poems with you when I couldn't always be there in person and always listening to my latest writing news.

To my siblings, for asking for poems for your weddings or accepting them for your birthday cards. I love sharing poetry with all of you.

To Traci Brimhall, for your advice, kindness, and mentorship over the years. Walking into your Introduction to Poetry Writing class at K-State was life-changing.

To the always glorious K-State English Department, past and present, including Karin Westman, Naomi Wood, Elizabeth Dodd, Katy Karlin, Traci Brimhall... you lead and inspire your students every day in writing and in life.

To our wonderful little poetry workshop, ENGL 763: I loved making blanket forts, going on road trips, and writing love notes with you.

To everyone who read versions of this manuscript and gave me feedback and advice: Hannah Jane, Dustin, Heather, and Sara. Without all of you, this finished piece wouldn't exist.

To Angel, and Kate, and everyone who has been a part of *elementia* over the years. Your belief in me since I was 14 has been unwavering, and has meant everything. Thank you for helping me realize I have a voice.

To everyone at *Poets Reading the News,* for years of collaboration and support. I've been so grateful to work with you and to be a part of your community and the space you've built.

To all the elementary and high school teachers who encouraged my love of reading and writing, including Mrs. Kolarik, Mr. O, Mrs. South, Mrs. Apprill, Mr. Benes, and Mr. Steinberg. I've been in your shoes at a school, now, so I know the relationships you built are invaluable.

To Kristy Nerstheimer, for being a great example to me as a writer and a teacher.

To everyone mentioned in these poems, for the love, and for being a part of my life. You add all the magic.

To my Aunt Annie, for being my book club buddy. Girls' Nights forever.

To Ross Gay, for always listening with intention, reading with tenderness, and writing with joy.

To the friends who've collaborated with me to make art— there's nothing better than creating with people I admire, whether in 8th grade or as an adult. Thank you also to all the friends who encouraged me to share my writing with others.

And lastly, thank you to all the family who have supported me. You help me land in a place of hope. I'm proud to carry our stories.

Table of Contents

1.

Wayfarer Memory / 1

roots and coffins / 2

i call the mountain mother / 3

kawaakari / 5

I ask the gingkos for forgiveness / 6

evacuation information / 7

Watching Itzhak Perlman Play "Theme
    from *Schindler's List*" / 9

where the strawberries grew / 10

Tableau After Sunset / 11

Surviving at Altitude / 12

It Blooms / 13

The Runner is Always Safe / 14

What I Did Instead of Dancing / 16

Landlocked / 18

The Air Was Heavy and the Days Were Long / 19

2.

hold fast and run like hell / 23

November 11, 2016: Poyntz Avenue / 24

to the yellow cardinal of alabaster, alabama / 25

the dragon and the one pound note / 27

A Day in Giverny / 28

Trinity / 29

Chorus of the Vanished / 30

What Comes Back / 33

Last Night on the Shores / 34

Vosges Mountains Interlude / 36

Outside Carl Sandburg's House / 37

I Leave Monet's *Water Lilies* at Every Shooting / 39

Lady of the Well / 41

streets of sun and memory / 42

Stage Magic / 43

lunar eclipse after rain / 44

An Hour at Orsay Station / 45

Beyond the Gates / 47

the days you were drowning / 49

3.

Fear as Metaphor / 53

Rationing Care / 54

Ars Poetica in the Emergency Room / 55

Simon / 56

ricepaper wings / 57

Twelve Days Pass Between the Death
    and the Funeral / 58

american gun violence as virus / 59

Living in Extremes / 60

Missouri Miles: The MR340 Begins / 61

my battery is low / 62

I want to mourn for you like the elephants mourn / 64

By Memory / 65

Quarantine: Years, Sinking / 66

Aubade to Kansas City / 67

We're Here Because / 68

4.

distilled / 71

For Leaving / 72

Like a Benediction / 73

What Doesn't Happen in Paris / 74

Of the Pleiades / 75

Succulents in Winter / 77

Wringing Myths from the Rain-Steeped New Year / 78

Ballad of Lightning / 80

Confessions From Tornado Alley / 82

So I Wouldn't Be Alone / 84

Soliloquy for My Eighteen-Year-Old Self / 85

Nocturne for the Baseball Streets / 87

Listening to "Stardust" by Artie Shaw & His Orchestra / 89

love notes and dissent / 90

golden shovel: election season / 92

the year of blessings and tenderness / 94

Ten Ways I Know I'm Alive / 97

Notes / 100

For my grandpa, Albert W. Strayhall,
For teaching me to tell stories.

"I'm not afraid of storms, for I'm learning how to sail my ship."

—Louisa May Alcott, *Little Women*

1.

Wayfarer Memory

My sister slipped into the car
with the ease of a traveler,
brushing the new year off her
shoulders in the highway dark.
She sang a skyscraper siren
song that made me miss the place
she used to be—the dependability
of the waves on the lakeshore;
city dawns and city dreams
and city nights on the balcony
as invisible stars blazed
on across light-years,
in spite of us. When she
laughed, I wondered at the
miracle of her next to me—
this woman who just minutes
ago was sweeping the clouds
through the sky. Chicago
lingered on her skin—in the
lightness of her bearing—and
I could sense its inky skyline
on her arm; in her mosaic heart.
To live divided, she knew, was
better than to never wander at all.
In the winter blackness, the car's
motion became the Orange Line L
lurching toward the city on a
sepia summer day. My sister
grinned at me, and I wished
that someday, I'd get to know
that coming home.

roots and coffins

at the cemetery / we set creamy pink / flowers above
my grandparents' / graves, whitman's grass grounding
/ our feet then / reaching down its roots / toward
heedless coffins // the earth was spinning us toward
sunset // for a / moment / we were silent, uttering
/ prayers inside our heads as / the water my father
poured over the graves / swept clear the markers and
/ our hearts // they lived through american dust /
europe's bones / a house they filled / together / fought
through the / blood and noise / and fears / of the
twentieth century

i turn // leave the neat grass / the disappeared water /
the distant dead / behind // i go forth to fight / for my
own century

i call the mountain mother

because i am desperate for something that
stands up to time. my mother as mountain is
something not forgotten. she touches clouds
with her exhales and is foundation as i sleep.

and if i call the river mother it is only to hear
her say that she is with me. my mother as river
laughs in shadow and sunlight. she carves her
path next to mine and sees me safely home.

and if i call the forest mother it's to see her
dance in cottonwoods. my mother as forest is
the swinging birches of poetry and trees of rest
and rootedness. she is fall brilliance afire in the sun.

and if i call the flowers mother it is to remember
their life-giving. my mother as flowers reaching is
the place i find peace again. she is glory in every
petal and the reason for green in this world.

and if i call the night my mother it is to know
her even far away. my mother as night listens
to my fears and starry wishes. she is comet tails
and meteors flying and gentle eclipse totality.

and if i call the dawn my mother it's to wake to
her each morning. my mother as the dawn is
gold light spreading; the tilt of my face to the
east. she is goodbye to darkness and chill.

and if i call the ocean mother it is to honor all i do
not know. my mother as the ocean is courageous
tides and steady lighthouse beams. she is point-of-
coming-home-to; port of memory.

and if i call the wind my mother it is to ask her to stay
with me. my mother as wind leaps over prairie hilltops
as easily as settling around my heart. she is the force that
i believe in.

kawaakari

there was a river / in the black hills / that my favorite
trail followed / with pine trees lining its banks / of hard
ground and towering rocks // i would beg my sister
/ to walk that trail as far as it went / as many days as
i could // and as we walked we would / recite poems
from memory / without ever missing a word // frost,
eliot, stevens / we filled the air / and our / hearts /
with their words / and i soaked up / nature, rhythm,
life // as the sun set / it would send sparks of water up
from the river / while our mother's birches / quiet and
true / led us home in the darkness

I ask the gingkos for forgiveness

on a Thursday morning. Half the leaves died
in the early frost. The other half are still yellow-
green, so I reach up and press the delicate fans

between my fingers. I feel each vein rough beneath
my skin. Once, when a nurse was drawing my blood,
she forgot her cotton ball to stop the bleeding. *Hold*

this, she said, leaving the needle in my arm. I looked
down at it in cold, flat wonder. Today I burn my candle
low until the wax is pooling. In church the other children

used to blow their flames out quickly, push their fingers in
the cooling wax. There's always something you don't need
to hold onto that lingers in your heart. November feels

like slowing down, like coming home, like our last stand
against the darkness blowing in on starving wind. Gradient
of sky, freeze my bones together. Trembling of fingers,

stay my hollow, ravenous blood

evacuation information

go now. leave unlocked
leave ready with
medicine with livestock
with shoes. remember
your pets. do not stop
to see the smoke pack
the sky the soaked sizzling
flames the ones who
run into ash. the resolute
fire that swallows them.

check which way the wind
is blowing. no telling when
you can return when you
can mourn what you will
find among the embers
and clouds. this is history.
this is now from trouble
and peaks to empty
trailheads blackened
creeks. snow sublimates
and the earth is dry dry
dry and the stars may as
well be a memory.

mountains heave under
garnet sky under air you
cannot breathe. looming
above is the shadowy

future, reeking of ozone;
leaping divides. the
slopes are vile beguiling
nightmares. all around you
the sirens are sounding.

your choice what to do
as the world is burning.
your eyes—closed or
open—when the
fire comes.

Watching Itzhak Perlman Play "Theme from *Schindler's List*"

With gentleness he rocks the melody through bow
and strings, follows each note to where it waits. A
sorrowing of ashes takes root within my chest.
History is no black and white remembrance on
a screen. It ascends; descends; plunges through
the dark. It grabs you. It makes of you a witness.

where the strawberries grew

they met / near the public library / my mother told
me // a slovenian / and an italian / came together as
/ our country stormed through war / and they had ten
children / and one they lost / and in a millennium / my
grandfather never saw / we drink / sicilian wine / eat
povitica / and my one-year-old nephew / will never
know them but / they are part of him still

one fall / i stood above two / rivers that came together
/ just like my grandparents did // accordion music
drifted / in the air / mixed with laughter and / the smell
of musty church basements / their frozen pasts / our
thawing futures and a / hundred years / of stories

on the hill's edge there stands / a twentieth century
monument: *to all / the immigrants*, its stone / words
read // for their dreams / for what they gave us / for our
tomorrows // for names now faded / for names living
on // for love, and for a / little boy growing / up on
strawberry hill / whose face i never saw

Tableau After Sunset

Bartle Hall's four pylons stand proudly, guarding us,
steel and concrete thrown skyward. The Power & Light
building offers a steady glow amidst the city's unassuming
rushing. Smolder and smoke drift through the night as
the Liberty Memorial illuminates the past. Trains bellow
through Union Station, full of noise and light and the
air of far-off places. Crown Center's fountains fly high,
dance cheerfully, ebb; reset. White-hot light chases around
the Western Auto arrow, completing the skyline once again.

Home: a Royals win,
I-70 dark, and fire-
works still in our eyes.

Surviving at Altitude

In the mountains I can't see ten
feet beyond the cabin's porch light
halo. Might've missed the stars out
there, just burning. The moths gather
in the night. Never fly again come
morning. This is a place I wake to
see the sunrise. In the smooth,
quick light, I like the way I look.
Storms kick up in the time I take
to shallow inhale. They whip upon
the rooftops, carve gouges in the
dirt, beat so loud we have to yell to hear
each other; to understand ourselves.
10,000 feet is foreign and cold. I walk
in the fog, in the rain, alone. I take
one hundred breaths. My chest
settles into aching. I watch my
sister dance in her wedding gown
with her laughing friends, their arms
secure around each other. They sway
to "Piano Man," surrounded by love and
promises and a bravery they found
in each other. I want that sheltered music.
That golden love is something I don't know.

It Blooms

My parents fly to Alaska at last when I am an ocean away
from them. I thought they'd never get there. Worried all
the doctor visits and lockdowns would ground them here
until they never got the chance to see those wilds together.
They call us as we rest in Paris' center, its angled streets
and measured rooftops and grey, sure stone surrounding us
like the mountains standing proud around them too. They
tell us about cloud-hidden peaks, midnight sun bus rides,
whales in the bay and fireweed everywhere, everywhere
the fires have touched. In London, amongst the wreckage
of the lightning war, they called it bombweed. Streets I
walked just days ago, cratered night after night after night—
but they refused to break. And in the craters of those nights—
flowers. Craters flush with flowers.

My parents walking trails of bombweed. My grandpas, too
young for dying, marching beneath those lightning-streaked
skies. And me, wending my way over brick and cobblestone
where smoke bloomed and flowers grew.

The Runner is Always Safe

The men are playing softball in the city park.
They know each other better than any scouting report—
know when to back up in the grassy outfield for the batter;
when to rush the throw; when to cheer or argue the calls.
The lime green ball fits in their palms as they tramp through
leaves, no responsibilities in that moment except to long
ballgames and the love that forms on the basepaths.
When bat clanks against ball, I see my Grandpa Willie
running through left field as fast as he can. His brothers
are running too—enough of them to fill a baseball team—
and none of them see 1940s Europe shadowing the horizon.
None of these men I never met—with infield dirt up and
down their bodies and grins tucked under their eyes—
see the looming tempest. It's just bats and gloves in the
afternoon and the neighborhood's parish bars at night as
Kansas City prepares to bid them goodbye. Oh, how their
parents and wives must have sat at darkened tables, so
many hearts an ocean away with guns in their hands and
prayers stitched into their uniforms. Oh, how their siblings
were so much alone as the hours stretched thin and the
weather turned.

Oh, the unnamable yearning when two brothers
unexpectedly embraced amidst the pall of boots and
barrels and the terror all around.

Oh, how the accordions sang out
from the Hill for their sons far away from home and all
they knew. Oh, how Union Station welcomed them home.

The ballplayers came back quiet, came back older,
came back. I walk in November next to the softball fields,
imagining what it sounded like when
my grandpa would laugh.

What I Did Instead of Dancing

*after Peace and Remembrance at the National World
War I Museum and Memorial*

The trains spark as they come around the curve, red-
    orange flashes
thrown wide 'round the metal rails beneath the concrete
    bridge.

Sometimes you have to slow down to really see. Beyond
    that
bridge are a hundred different crowds, shifting and
    shouting and

laughing through these years. Many times I've stood
    beneath the
Memorial's tower and watched the lights blink on.
    The lamps burn

onward after sunsets. They cast shadows on us all.
    The enduring notes
of "Taps" linger on the hilltop. The trumpet gleams like
    smoothed and melted

starlight. Its music calls all home. The Great War ended
    a century ago
and now I stand in its echo on the frost-touched lawn.
    No crowds

come. The air is the depths of cold that you feel to the
    marrow. Inside

the Station, jazz music is swinging and ringing and
    filling the cavernous

rooms—every single person made into light. Somewhere
    in there my brother
and his wife are dancing, gilded in Glenn Miller and
    suspenders and pearls.

Away from the midnight-ready clock face I walk, out to
    the wintering
air. Alone I watch the cycling projection spiral outward
    across the

Great Frieze, curl up the resolute tower.
    An eruption
of poppies. A blooming of poetry. A
    summoning of peace.

Landlocked

After my grandpa died, someone asked if he
had suffered. I paused in shock—blinking, asked
to interrogate my grief. Wondered how to
answer without giving the tangled mess of my
heart away. I think I have offered enough. I
am tired of treading water in this landlocked
city. When the weather warms I watch clouds
building in the evening. The frogs croak loudly
as the night gets still and cool. I cannot settle
on a single thing. Can't tune the world enough
to focus on the skipping of my heart. I think of
Ross Gay's care in every word he read upon an
April stage, my friend beside me in a college town
that's not our own. We hug before we say goodbye
on the roof of the parking garage. I write the names
of ones I'm missing on my slightly sunburned skin.
I promise myself I'll call when things are better.

The Air Was Heavy and the Days Were Long

A child in summer understands the meaning of life:

barefoot, playing hide and seek til the sun goes down,
crickets sounding in the darkness,
dust caking her feet; she smiles and
eats marmalade on toast in the mornings,
feeling the freedom in an empty day.

Gazing at the crumpled clouds from the top of a hill,
her hands restlessly pick at the hem of her shirt where
    the thread's coming undone.
In the shade of trees she reads well-worn books,
July days passing with the turning pages.

Kansas girl feels the air crackle as
lightning splinters the black ceramic sky.
Miles away from home, as the day becomes
night, she doesn't flinch at the thunder.
Over tangled roots she races, through
pouring rain and seas of mud.

Quiet comes to her mind;
revisiting the sunset in her memories,
singing to herself as the shadows stretch out
    across the ground,
then turning toward the sky, staring
upwards at pinprick stars and planets.

Venus is on her mind, unreachable

when her eyes slip closed—

except in her dreams, she can grab the flickering,
    fiery stardust,

yesteryear's light sparking as she

zips a handful in her jacket pocket.

2.

hold fast and run like hell

when you could jump / the trains, grandpa said / you
could go / anywhere

well, as long as you were / home for dinner // as long
as you came home / to marceline before the / night
moved on / without you // as long as you were fast /
enough to leap / aboard the heaving / pounding train
cars / you could go beyond / your familiar street / your
mother's voice / the dust of coal mines dense / in the
small town shadows / find a freedom you / wanted
from the very earnestness of / your heart // before
your town was / main street, usa / before you were a
/ soldier / husband / father / widower / grandfather
who taught me poker / and to love as fiercely / as
gently / as unflinchingly / as i could

it was the trains that would / one day claim your father
/ a railyard accident // but somehow, even after / the
grief / the trains still made you / think of freedom

November 11, 2016: Poyntz Avenue

The Friday after, I take time I don't
have to hear poems and prose bounce
off gallery walls. All around me are
people trying desperately to find beauty
again. Words echo, enter welcoming ears,
and I think that as long as people like this
exist, and speak, and mourn and unite in
"Hallelujah" light, we'll find our way again.
Fear and uncertainty press against
sheltering window glass, but tonight,
we refuse to let them in. We lost, so
there's pain in our grief-creased faces;
real sorrow that so many people voted
for hate. But together we laugh. Together,
we trade storied words, and our words
unfold new stories. Every syllable weighs
heavy with endings and beginnings. And I
am not silent like I have been in the past.
I have my pen—my paper—my voice.
I stand, and do not shake, and offer my
love out to the world.

to the yellow cardinal of alabaster, alabama

1. bird of paradise in an alabama backyard
with your feathers of honey, you shine
quietly amidst the crimson. beware:
swarms of bullets buffet the air beneath
your cherished wings. you cannot stop flying,
Huma, because there are no more safe
places to land. the canaries all are dead
now. we ignored them as they fell out of
the sky like leaden yellow raindrops,
like the locusts of exodus, like brilliant, little,
once-breathing meteorites.

2. bird of compassion, we need you
in this aphotic darkness—in this absence
of right. instead of throwing
prized pennies into wishing wells, our
children are being buried beneath numb
earth and palls of periwinkle. the day
seventeen more lives were stolen in
florida, you still lived in anonymity; flew
unweighted and free. then we were all
again eclipsed in bloody, breath-stealing
shadow.

3. bird of spirit and blessings, please
share with us your secrets of survival.
our wings have rotted and we can't
seek your sky as sanctuary—we must
live in this bittersweet world with

our feet firmly planted between guns
and gravestones. give us hope in your
gold-dusted beauty, and the miraculous
courage to sing songs of our own. now is
the time of the lionhearted—now we rise
from the fire to fight.

the dragon and the one pound note

emergency // a promise // a one pound note, blue and
orange, colors / quieted by the decades / a shadow on
my grandpa's wall so / fragile between my fingers and
it / sends me to the weeping past / to men / to boys
/ stuck in the nazi muck / where mines leapt up and /
mortars screamed / down and the boys prayed not for /
glory but just to see / the morning, said / goodbyes they
hoped they'd / never need // where the hürtgen forest
devoured / them all, and blood was in the / everywhere
/ and my grandpa walked / alone

except for those beside him // boys with a one / pound
note / placing pen to english paper / signing their names
to memory / there's ink spot / rebel / gi smith / tex
and red / and grandpa sodbuster / missouri boy in the
middle of another / continent, in the middle of / this
one pound / note, surrounded by names that would
never / be together again / their ink bleeding through /
to st. george and / his winged foe from the tales of old
and

my grandpa tucked / that one pound / note into his
pocket / as he prepared to charge / the dragon fire

A Day in Giverny

from inside the Nelson Atkins Museum of Art

You have to wake before the dawning. You have to be
　　willing to live in darkness for a little. Art comes softly
like grey after grey before sun ever leaps the horizon.
　　Sometimes I don't move for

an entire day. I acquaint myself with hints of blue; with
　　birdsong early as always; with the fullness of light and
sound in the air and water. Sunlight washes color out like
　　paint upon a

palette upon my arm upon my skin. And beneath the
　　leaves I see the water. And beneath the colors, I see
the blooms. I imagine what filters below the surface–blue
　　purple green dream.

Aftermath of rain. Waterdrops when ducks take wing
　　for evening. This is a peace I would die to keep forever.
Evening takes hold. Evening holds me. Dusk, bring your
　　pinks and your fadings.

White petals ripple under moonlight. Water ripples white
　　under my boat. Soon all that's left will be bright beating
starlight. Look backward at the water. Look unflinching at
　　the night. Colors in

the black. Violets 'neath the moon. Crickets in the grass
　　and the reeds. To paint is the greatest answered prayer.
Night grows stronger. Flowers fold. Then the cold. The
　　cold. The cold.

Trinity

Fields of gypsum. Endless dunes. A white and sandy
sea. Beneath our car there is no road, only hard-packed
grains of crystalline infinity. Some animals that live here
live only here. Born here. Fly here. Die here. They see
the mountains in the distance; they see the sand-blown
sky; they call it theirs, forever. The wind blows hard and
unrelenting, a sandscreen in the air. In this place no
shadow ever comes easily. Brightness stretches for miles,
commanding, punishing. The sun will take us if we let
it, if we let our guard down in the light. I race down
dunes and shut my eyes. Make angels for a moment.
I set my feet. I claw back upwards. Start the cycle once
again. Nearby, machines of war send casual missiles
screaming through the air–the eternal test for peace.
Moths scatter over empty dune fields next to mushroom-
clouded sky. Fly here. Die here.

Chorus of the Vanished

Velvet curtains open on the grand stage of the European
Theater; the stage of broken countries and bombed-out
cities and cattle cars rattling on train tracks to Hell, and
no matter how thick the blood or how overwhelming the
rubble or how acrid the air, the show must go on.

Enter: Stage left, a boy from Marceline, Missouri,
who grew up jumping trains with his little brother,
and whose first campaign was on the roads of his
hometown in the neighborhood rubber gun wars.

Cue: The tall sodbuster soldier with a bloody bucket
on his shoulder marches through the wreckage
of Omaha Beach, and the days that follow are loud
with machine gun fire and littered with fallen friends,
and the boy digs a slit trench like the others
as the mortars and artillery shells rain down,
and they survive by burying themselves alive.

Center stage: In 1944, the boy is hit, and the audience
holds its breath as blood covers his face, and as the fight
continues he is alone on the stage, his solitary footsteps
scuffling along until he finally happens upon help, and he
is pitied by the other wounded because the mortar shell
didn't do the kind of damage that would send him home.

Tableau: Trees so thick they block the sun on chilly,
worthless days; splintering wood flying through the air;
fog and rain and the boy is lost, and every step he takes

he fears a Bouncing Betty mine will leap out of the ground and end him, and he slogs through the mud, and they all leave the wounded behind because the fighting won't stop and the Hürtgen Forest opens up and swallows them whole.

Intermission: Only, really, in this play there is no break, because sleep is just as haunting as reality, and closed eyes can't hide the burning stench of cordite or the miasma of wrecked bodies in a ruined tank, and screams mix with the screech of artillery, and the man from Missouri has to do his best to sleep while the gunshot sky is falling.

Tragedy: At the back of the stage, the audience can see the man and his company, and they can see his face set to obey the order to hold their position no matter what, and he says his goodbyes because to fight with them has been a privilege, and his head is bowed and his fists are clenched as he imagines his family receiving the unwanted, undeniable telegram, until—

Crisis: Averted, and new orders come, and the men move out. In the freezing cold foxholes, even as the man and his platoon fear the worst from the New Year, he receives a surprise: star shells fired high into the night by the enemy, a gesture they are happy to return as they consider that for one night, they understand each other: far from home, terrified and sad and tired, deciding to live one night in peace.

Denouement: He parades through Colmar with his division, and the city is liberated, and as 1945 slips by, they all hope victory is near. News of VE day is greeted with bubbles of golden champagne, and his job may not be done, but the curtain is coming down, and this fight is almost over.

Ghost light: Even when the theater empties, and the blood dries, and the man's feet touch Missouri soil, and he is home, the ghost light stays on, because the ones lost will always be there in the darkness—dog tags glimmering

What Comes Back

after Couple in the Tuileries Garden, Paris, 1945

The chairs are lined up on the barren path. Pile of rubble
rests right of the focal point. In the distance, dust and
smoke make outlines hazy. No flowers in the gardens,
but sitting side-by-side is beauty enough for now.
Maybe the world is still falling apart. Maybe all their
family is gone, gone to places they can never return
from. Maybe. But the chairs are wiped clean with a
handkerchief anyway. Coats are pulled tighter around
shoulders as they face what is lost forever. Hands are
linked together like a prayer. Anchors: a comforting arm;
a straight back; steely eyes the camera never sees. In the
future, flowers grow here. And fountains flow and people
smile and the trees give shade and the air is clear and
French flags fly free in the sun. For now, it's swept-aside
rubble. It's love planted along the walkways until laughter
can grow. A whisper starts within the garden; is shared
between the couple; flies throughout the city on
triumphant wings: *Fluctuat nec mergitur.*
Tossed by the waves,
but never sunk.

Last Night on the Shores

Steps descending into lapping ink. Maze of alleys. Maze
    of tides. Maze of truths.
A train speeds me across the expanse of salt and blue and
    real, and at the end

I throw out my arms because all roads lead to water. My
    sister and I cradle finest
glass between our fingers; choose, like our sister before us,
    which flame-forged pieces

should sit beside our hearts. Burgundy leather roars
    beneath our hands. We
take up masks to become strangers to each other. Twice
    we pass the Bridge of Sighs,

breathing freely in the heat of open air. The Venice night
    sits contentedly around us,
heavy with all the years that it remembers. A watermelon
    blessing leaves us smiling.

Across the lagoon, Giudecca's solitary paths will always
    know how immemorial I felt there—
that place I existed alone. The layered peace. I shake
    myself before I leave that divinity of

quiet behind for the future to love. The lagoon sunset
    reminds me how far I am from home,
my face draped in unfamiliar winds as water leaps through
    the windows. Tonight, all is

linked. Tonight, a floating city conjures a bridge across
    the waves. Tonight, fireworks
blanket the sky, clapping across canals, sending shadows
    after footsteps after dreams

I didn't believe in. Lanterns lead the way to where those
    dreams have wings. Between
defiant buildings the dark combusts with color. I sit
    upon an ancient well and imagine

who once drank there. All the wonder in the world and
    I want to set it down. Before I
trace the ash-tinged water along the Redeemer's night, I
    slip the mask once more to

my face. Black ribbon tangles in my hair;
    music notes cut across
my cheek. My features, unmooring. My lips,
    red and still.

Vosges Mountains Interlude

The train platforms in Alsace are silent. At peace. Across
the tracks a stork stands proudly on a lamppost, centered
in the calm. The stream slips carefully onward beneath
contented pink flowers, near vineyard rows growing lush
on the hillsides. Staring down the Vosges Mountains on
a brilliant Bastille Day, it's hard to call to mind my grandpa's
most enduring memories of those slopes. Simply put: It
was the cold. The snow. The burning skin in the icy air;
the stab of every heaving step through weighted, heaping
drifts. They waded through the white, grateful for the
depth that kept the mines at rest in frozen ground.
Even then, the half-timber buildings they fought through
were old. They were old when my grandpa raced from
one street corner to the next, February a stranglehold
around him as 1945 trudged on. They were old when he
slept in their empty shells and when he paraded through
the Alsace streets in victory, so much older than when he
first reached those shores only months before. Today, the
red keystone on the wall signals I'm right where I was always
meant to be. For my grandpa standing in that spot, the
war was almost over. Lorraine Cemetery was almost full.

Outside Carl Sandburg's House

after Carl Sandburg and Nelson Algren

It's October, and like Algren promised, Chicago whispers.
Chicago sings. Chicago bites with blood dripping and fists
curled and eyes that look straight through you. Today, on
my 25,000th step, Ravenswood's sidewalks open up in
this place that was just beyond my heart all along, streets
from, once, my sister's home. One hundred years ago, the
poet, Sandburg, walked here; held his wife here; kissed
his daughter's head here. Here the city was alive and
cursing and laughing in the century new. Here a man
reckoned with destiny as the people spoke around him,
trains coursing like veins before wars and pandemics
and Pulitzers, decades after the fire. When I shout atop
Chicago skyscrapers built by Chicago hands or dodge
vibrant crowds in one hundred different motions,
Sandburg's pen dogs my heels; straightens my slipping
shoulders. *Know this place I loved*, he says, *and listen
to its people all.* Jack-o-lanterns gleam on iron railings
nearby. The buses sprint past on this weekday eve. The
light is going out of the day when I see it: This is a porch
city. A lighthouse on the shore city. A rain until your socks
are wet, pound your sneakers up metal L steps, close your
eyes on the rooftop and listen for all you're worth city.
It's eight illuminated floors of library books and bridges
pointed up at the brilliant sky and the Red Line every
fifteen minutes through every one of my dreams. It's a
people whose neighborhood's everything city and a sing
in subway tunnels city and a sit on the Pilsen sidewalk city,
even with strangers, even on a humid summer day. On a

last night in the city October evening, I leave Graceland's graves and Diversey's boats and Lincoln Park's Lily Pool in my past, my future. I speak Carl Sandburg from the dirt with my sister at my back, in the only voice I have, in the city I wish about. And Chicago–she speaks back, knuckles taped and ready, thundering through my skin; my calloused fingers.

I Leave Monet's *Water Lilies* at Every Shooting

Everywhere I turn, the water goes
on. It goes on for years, and the
petals open and close and open,
and every day the sun on the
soft water looks different to my
dying eyes. If I paint the right
ray of sun I just know I will
open a doorway to a world
beyond this aching night.

When I paint, I feel the wind
sweep over my lips. The colors
are overbright but they are
truer than in any of my dreams.
Short brushstrokes. Slack
outlines. Just raindrops of
sunlight and the unstoppable
motion of this broken joyful
disappearing life.

From beneath the water,
lily pads are the clouds
in my sky. They are the
unbreakable surface, but
still I am never drowning—
only learning to live under-
water, painting fish scales
on my skin. I will not give
up wonder for anything.

So I place water lilies into
machine gun barrels. I
drip paint through the cities
and past the gates of
our cemeteries. I feel the
seasons changing with the
shifting in the air. And when
the shadows grow darker,
I paint my lantern bright.

Lady of the Well

Today, living is not a burden. The
sunset on the Tiber isn't spectacular
or immaculate or the most beautiful
I have ever seen, but it has a heft to
it. I walk halfway across a bridge and
think about goodbyes. Rome tolls
its secrets in the summer, in the
cooling air, in quiet. On the way
last night, I happened upon a miracle.
I stood somewhere they say Santa Maria
touched. Imagine one soft blessing, one
well of water, as enough to cure your
weeping heart. The hills ring. The bells
are silent. The fountains rush with the
promise I make to carry myself back
here one day. At the river, I pray for
healing. Eternity is in the water here.

streets of sun and memory

sicilia / island of a thousand souls // you were sappho's /
place of exile // you felt the footsteps of / the ancients
/ dragged through civilizations until / you emerged
once more / stronger than ever // sicilia / bloodshed
cannot have you / sicilia / the facists cannot have you /
sweet sicilia / mount etna and typhon cannot drag you
to the depths // sicilia, you are autonomous / you are
proud / you are queenly / you are the watcher on the
/ mediterranean sea / lighthouse of the old country
// sicilia, you are the grapes that / grow in your avola
vineyards / you are medusa's / head staring boldly back
/ you are my ancestors' resting place my / family i have
never seen / you are the sun / falling faithfully on via
cuttitta

Stage Magic

after William Shakespeare

At the Globe, I let my eyes close in the still
summer shade. I focus on my breaths, let Shakespeare's
words slide across my skin. To my right a young
woman follows along with *Lear* in her hands, tracking
projected words with steady movements. I gaze
across the groundlings shifting subtly on the floor.
One viewer watches with delight as Gloucester's
eyes are gouged. It's bloody and sure and a thrill
of horror on the stage. Sweetened, cloud-patched
blue peeks in through the thatched roof circle as the
audience becomes part of the show. Edmund
makes the people laugh with his repartee on
romance; Kathryn Hunter's Lear commands
the mighty storms. Even weary I watch, enraptured,
as the play's final words are spoken and the
dance begins. The whole audience is clapping,
and the actors' feet are circling, and all our joy is
flying. This is theatre come alive. After the show, I
exit the Wooden O, a parting and a sorrow. Heavy
doors and iron gates swing shut. I wait for my
sister on the steps beside the Thames and watch the
actors quietly meld into the crowd, one after the other.
A touch of magic swirls around them in the late-day
London light. I am worn down. I am jetlagged. I, too,
am magic alive

lunar eclipse after rain

my family gathers in the hospital parking lot. we don't
know yet that in a few months we'll be back there again.
but this time, we stay outside in the may air, staring past
streetlights to the early summer celestial show. we spread
a blanket on the ground and laugh as sun, earth, and
moon align. this isn't the first time we've gone chasing
the heavens, decades-old binoculars in our hands or a
well-loved telescope at our sides. in colorado we stood
on the pitch-black porch and held each other close in
the mountain night. we followed wheeling stars until
our fingers numbed and we had to retreat to the cabin's
sanctuary warmth. we tucked blankets around each other
and questioned constellations. the mountains
raised us closer to the disappearing light. back home
we say goodbye beneath the red moon gazing. while
the light is gone, so much is hidden. so much is made
anew.

An Hour at Orsay Station

The statues pose half-dressed in afternoon summertime
    light. Fabric falls
across their bodies in smooth soft shifting marble.
    Eternal flowers in their hair.
Heads in their hands after decades of sighing, visitors
    sifting around them: gods

and saints and poets and queens and me. Above us the
    clock swings on—a
window out, a warning within: our time is running
    short. When I shut my eyes
against the countdown it's like I can hear the Seine
    pushing past me. I can

feel the thundering of trains shaking through Gare
    d'Orsay. It tolls through all
these years. Beneath the grandest art are walls that said
    welcome home to war's
losthearted. Terminal of us—the end; the
    stopping place

My feet my heart my artist's hands take me to a storied,
    starried night. The Rhône
is every color Vincent dreamed it could be. The minute
    hand slashes onward.
Vincent's translation of the world is real before me. He
    figured out how to wrest

down the stars; how we can light the dark if we try.
   Tick. His Paris was sharp and
lilting and barred and lost and swirling cold. It leaks in
   through the vaulted ceilings;
settles on harried, beauty-struck crowds. Vincent and I
   spend dwindling seconds

getting the shadows in our hearts just right

I back away from the darkness. *Tock.* I rush past countless
   post-Impressionism
masterpieces; the world begins to blur around me. Gallery
   doors swing shut behind.
I pass a bloody Paris; a foggy cathedral; frothing waves
   and an ocean bigger

than us all. Outside, the sun is high. Metal flowers climb
   stonework, always
light-seeking. The clock's gaze is steady. I try to remember
   the stars.

Beyond the Gates

The land of the dead is green and lush and full of leafy
    shadows.
I turn. Another angel. I turn. Another sword. I turn.
    Another set
of stony wings. Across the street, a burial; an opening;
    an exhale

of the earth. Free of the weight of that grief and the
    slow walk to
the grave, our little group of strangers wanders western
    pathways
to the cadence of quiet stories. We pass a lead-lined
    coffin; weave

the winding Circle of Lebanon; enter the dank of the
    locked-up
catacombs where patches of light guide our steps beside
    moldering
caskets. Over us, stained-glass hymns echo out of St.
    Michael's. For

280 years, a cedar towered above it all—now it, too, has
    gone to rest.
Inverted torches burn brightly in metal and stone; light
    the way to
something they hoped would be better. I think I could
    walk these paths

forever. I could visit the dead and see the seasons change
    around them—
mud form above them; the stillness of snow or the
    brightness of ferns turning
golden in the autumn. I could play the stone piano and
    read poetry to the

poets gone before me. 53,000 graves. Three times
    as many
bodies. Thousands who loved and lost them, even
    the ones
without a marker to show they once were here.
    I turn. Ivy and

flowers grow above them, moss and weeds and lamb's ear,
    currant
and honey and rouge amidst the wild forest and the stony
    dirt. The
leaves unfurl. They breathe
    again.

the days you were drowning

this summer the air sits heavy,
but with none of the gold-tinged
wonder of past remembrances.
my mother to the doctor; my
country to the edge; my own
heart stagnant after years of
desert-living. so, one night, we
sang songs out open windows and
drove beneath july-black skies
because i swore the comet was
waiting for us at the end of a
missouri road. we stood on
shadow gravel and i willed the
clouds to clear. finally, binoculars
and patience opened our skies
to universal divinity. on the
partly-cloudy backroads with a
little too much light, neowise
might have been a smudge of star;
an interstellar patchwork of awe
and luminosity. a piece of life i
had never seen before; will never
see tomorrow

3.

Fear as Metaphor

On Thursday mornings I drive through the sunshine
to get coffee to-go before work. It's cold but I roll the
window down anyway, feel the thawing air on my
fingertips. Winter hurts more than I'm saying to anyone.
Every piece of happiness is weighted down. At night
I work alone with books stacked tall around me. The
spines are cold no matter how long I hold them in my
hands. I turn the lights off and leave the shelves to speak
to moonlight. Every time I talk with someone there's a
truth I refuse to voice: I don't think I was made to hope
for the best. I give my love to dying plants and paper
cranes and the annotations I scrawl in poetry books.
I buy myself flowers to coax colors back into the year.
I'm tired in a way that freezes the heart. I wear pearl at
my throat to capture all the light I can. Every day I'm
more afraid of what may come. I'm trying to say *this is
dragging me to the depths*. I'm trying to say *I love you
and I'm afraid*. I'm trying to say *my hands won't warm
anymore*.

Rationing Care

One cloudy April afternoon I task
myself with triage. Push down the
pains I can't afford today. I cut my hair
to change something, to wake up different
than the sleepless mornings come before.
I picture my fist meeting brick; the wild
power in my wind-up, the bloody scrape
of desperation through my clenched-tight
knuckles. The weather calls for sun but
it's only getting darker outside. Every month
my mom's doctor tells her what the cancer
antigen measures in her blood. My family tells
me it's all one day at a time. Survive first,
ask questions later. Tornado sirens are sounding
to the storm-dark west. I ask the ones I love if
they're sheltering; if they can hear the
crescendoing of warning. I open my
window as the thunder sounds

Ars Poetica in the Emergency Room

In the emergency room, I think
that I've been a bad poet.

I promised I'd write one poem each day in
April—but I've been tired and there is so often
pain during this National Poetry Month. Here
they can scan me like a barcode, and I admire
their efficiency while hating my machine
opticality, laying there in my second hospital
gown of the day. When I told the doctor I wasn't
pregnant he laughed and said *we'll see*.
There's an acrostic on the wall that spells SPEAK UP
and a baby crying down the hall and there are clear,
hydrating fluids flowing into my arm and maybe
my cat is asleep, home under the covers, and maybe
I should've tried to outlast the mind-blankening pain
so I wouldn't owe thousands in hospital bills, and I
wonder if the other poets have trouble writing, too,
with a blood pressure cuff on one arm
and an IV in the crook of the other, heart rate
monitor clipped lovingly to their index fingers.
I want to leave here and sculpt this poem into
something beautiful, or honest. To keep these
candid words and this intimate, delicate heart.

When my phone autocorrects poet to power, I think
maybe I've been doing something right after all.

Simon

Our cat used to sit in our windowsills, whiskers
pressed close to the screens. His eyes followed
every darting grey squirrel, every blade of grass,
every cardinal on the swinging power line. We
sometimes clipped on his collar and let him prowl
the backyard with commanding grace. He would
roll in the empty garden dirt or press the catmint
flat beneath his back, its blossoms purple and
fragrant around him, or just close his eyes against
the perfect feeling of afternoon sunlight warm upon
his fur. Sometimes when he lay down in the still-
warm, freshly laundered sheets, I'd stretch out next
to him and place my face against his side, his breaths
and heartbeats so much quicker than my own. Before
he died we let him sit outside again. It was late July
and time to go. I ran my hand along his soft, striped
head. I made sure he wasn't alone. In the shafted light,
I still see pawprints on the pavement. In the catmint—
lavender budding. Solace in the bloom.

ricepaper wings

in this box i find / fifty years of remembrance //
letters that waved their paper / wings over the sea
/ across the world // i want to cradle them / each
unfolded page / each happy birthday long / forgotten
// before your hair turned silver / before we knew /
each other's faces / before our final / january goodbye
// what did you think / when you opened the wispy
mobile / set its fragile figures free?

your pen pal smiles / from her boat / young girl in /
faded grey / and black / and decades / long behind
us / and i wonder / if she knows / somehow / you're
gone

Twelve Days Pass Between the Death
and the Funeral

It's spring. My grandfather died last Thursday.
We knew it was coming. He was not alone. But all
I can think of is the coming heft of the coffin. The
poetic drape of the flag. His hand in my hand in the
too-bright ICU, squeezing. Plastic rosary beads nestle in
my pocket like coins for the ferryman. My sister-in-law
hugs me with all the love in this world. My coworker
says *you seem quiet today*. My grandpa's handwriting
stares up at me from the photocopied funeral plan. I
press my fingers to the paper and imagine I can feel
the indent of his pen. I say I would do anything for
him. I hold a piece of paper listing everyone he loved
and how to reach them. What a bittersweet blessing,
to recognize the end. What heart scraped-raw and
grievous. My shoulders tense with the weight of oceans;
with the density of a neutron star; with the crush of
sky on an astronaut returned to rain-dark, fresh-tilled
dirt. I never thought I would carry you.

american gun violence as virus

oh beloved oh lost oh my
body dragged down as
it spreads. it spreads. it spreads.

school yards school drills school screams
empty thoughts empty prayers empty actions
it spreads. it spreads. it spreads.

small coffins medium coffins large coffins
festering hearts calcifying hearts still hearts
it spreads. it spreads. it spreads.

is this america? this is america? america is this.
nothing is poetry nothing is holy nothing is safe
it spreads. it spreads. it spreads.

from the earth upon the earth to the earth
like blood like grief like pain
it spreads. it spreads. it spreads.

oh beloved oh heartsick oh my
raging, tear-soaked fight–
it spreads. it spreads. it spreads

Living in Extremes

This year the leaves died brown on the trees. Frost
came too quick; droughts held on too long. The wetlands
have no water for the birds passing through the sky.
We live in fear of early snow and the cold that grips on
tightly. November isn't supposed to be this way. Heavy
is the snow that falls on us. The wind descends. Night
comes early now.

Missouri Miles: The MR340 Begins

We wake before the sun can rise. The July morning
promises thick heat and sweltering hours. In the
sleepiness of the city we walk like dreamers down
the covered Town of Kansas bridge, day breaking
around us. Below, the Missouri is merciless, its
channels always shifting, its churn chasing waves
along the shores. Other faithful gather around us
to stand witness to a voyage just beginning. The
deep blue sky is scored with light as the first
boats round the bend, paddles flashing furiously
and water whipping through the air. We wave and
cheer as the river guides them beyond our sight,
far from loved ones and safe harbors and easy
nights. They are somewhere I have never known,
paddling through stars and fog and sweeping sunsets,
always away, always east, always wild with love—
only the river remembering what they speak to the
currents.

my battery is low

and it's getting dark. it has all gone
dark. there is a cold seeping
through wire veins to the center of me.

dust chokes out the stars. the wind
offers no forgiveness, and so i anchor
myself and begin to dream.

i dream of fire, of heat so blazing i was
born again; of what you pray for
when you're falling.

i dream of where the land was
hollowed out into nothing; of the
impacts that came before me.

i dream of sols when i was lost, or trapped,
or could not remember myself. i dream of
someone who reached through

the years to always bring me back. i
dream of places only my shadow has
touched. of waking up to the

kiss of sunlight. and i dream of
loss. of looking backward. of the
hush that comes when you become

alone. i dream of miles behind me and
one-way trips and of gypsum glinting
through rust-rose dust. i dream

wonder and discovery and of
doing what's impossible; of the grace
of beautiful and proud desolation.

sometimes in my dreams i hear
music playing. it sounds muffled, like
a phonograph underwater, or a melody

caught in static. beneath the
music, i hear voices. the louder i
try to answer them, the softer

they get. a calm settles. i dream
of cornflower sunsets. i dream of
light returning

(For Opportunity)

I want to mourn for you like
the elephants mourn

to lift up your blank bones and press
you close to my heart. I want to
anchor your floating ribs to my arms as I
march beneath the sun-white sky
with dust-marbled skin and grass
slivering blood down my legs.

I want to say your name to the shadows
and stand in silence amidst your ashes,
because I still hear you laughing somewhere
I can't see. I want your veins to bracelet
my wrist because maybe then I will still
feel your heartbeat flush against my pulse.

I want to go to the last place I remember you.

By Memory

after Aimee Nezhukumatathil and Katherine Riegel

I don't want anger in my garden. It grows well enough in
my chest, tucked amongst ribs and lungs and wild,
sparking nerves. Give me fiercest wind and labyrinthine
days before the bloom. On the way home from school
we used to drive by honeysuckle, slow down and breathe
the happy chaos on the fence, yellow blanketing metal
above the chipping concrete and golf-green grass. Other
evenings we'd spot Rose of Sharon on our walks—
a plant with both my mother and me within it, tangled
in flowers forever. Last week, I went to the garden every
day. Saw an afternoon turn dark with thunder; lightning
drowning in the downpour. My mom and I took shelter
from the storm beneath the earth. The heavens let loose
upon our heads. For every season, there is a heartbreak.

Spring is fear and hope
and memorizing every
face of ones you love

Quarantine: Years, Sinking

Lockdown wearing on. Spring
deepening. A kindness of
strawberries. Grass is growing
taller than our bodies. I sit
with cactus blooms. With
columbine. With yuccas and
the dawn. Sunflowers whisper
in the dark. Year's past. Years
past. Years passed. Colder air;
same aches. Say ghosts are in
these walls. Dying stars and
dying years. After flames, the
heat lingers; refuses to let go.

Aubade to Kansas City

There is a part of me that will never leave you.
Part of me will always be here—in the strawberries
that thrive by the river; in the fountains that laugh
in the springtime; in the baseballs that sail out
into the night. You have given me the feet I
stand tall with; the heart I love well with; the
strength I can leave with. And what more
is there I can say to thank you for all the
years you've loved me? For making me
a child of two places; a woman of cities
that can still look up to the stars at night?

There is no goodbye that must come
between us. No goodbye because I
still will see you when I close my eyes—
your ready skyline; your Main Street
shine. And I hear your stormy jazz like
a music box winding down; I feel your
embrace in the glimmering symphony
notes trailing out from the Kauffman.
When the dawn comes, this is what I
promise to remember: blue confetti
rain, the streetcar ringing out, and
Loose Park's cherry blossom joy,
wishing me happiness

We're Here Because

In Brick Lane, the kaleidoscope lights blur their blues
and prismatic hues as they crisscross cobblestone streets
in the summer night. I never thought I'd be here, in this
place I saw on pages in a hallowed college classroom.
Never knew I'd have the courage to step into the sky,
to leap oceans with outstretched wings. London carries
surprises in its heart, in its graffitied walls and sun-loved
streets and the sheer aliveness in the evening air. And
now I know I can leave my home. And now I know I
can face my worst but make it through. And when I drag
my body to tomorrow, when I bruise my hands on stone
and brick and wipe some blood off of my cheek, there'll
be sunflowers in Van Gogh yellow on the wall. There'll
be warm tea to soothe my sorest throat, and my sister's
mug clinking mine in the hotel lobby. In my bones I
know this city like this city knows the flame—like an
old embrace. Here I am: brave, and wonderous, and
wreathed in crucible fire.

4.

distilled

what if my loneliness was framed for
gallery walls? my feet fall with the
cadence of a mourner, of mornings, of
more to the world than loss and fear and
my one bloody, tripping heart. but i am
not the empty museum halls or the sweetness
of a memory. if peace is what you're
looking for, you can't find it breathing
backward. give me the lover in brownstone,
writing for his city. i want the sundressed
smiling traveler and coffee ice cream
in the nighttime and for my paint-chipped
nails and crooked fingers to reach for
every breeze. if the world is art and love
and wonder, then i want to be it all—the
song-filled vineyard on a summer evening;
the one who clasps a hand in the dark.
i want the intimacy of springtime, of a
mother, of the iris bulb beating beneath
the rain-soaked earth. if the world is
not easy, then dress me like a prizefighter,
like a poet, like someone who bends their
bitterness into swing after swing after swing.

For Leaving

My cup steams furiously in the coffee shop.
The rain is cold, is unforgiving. I question
every changing of the seasons. Divide my
life into quarters and wonder how many years
each gets. Rain is good weather for leaving
behind. I search for what to write in years
washing out the sky. I want to say my goodbyes
to deep unhappiness, to miseries of the heart.
Some days I forget my tea until it's long gone
cold. I let my body split itself apart. Heat seeps
into my aching fingers. It's easy to say
I wish that things were different.

Like a Benediction

I am one who has screamed for my city. I have stood
tall down the third base line as the sky turned gold
turned pink turned ink and the baseball-round moon
rose. I have watched the flags turn, felt the wind shift,
breathed in the sudden swirl of a towering storm and its
chaos of lightning and cloud-quaking, seat-shaking
thunder, Missouri torrents backlit by stadium lights
and the scoreboard crown electric in the swoop of
darkness. I have turned my face to the soft touch of
spring sunshine, extended my hand over the slick metal
railing, felt the fountain spray light on my skin. It's cool
and quiet like a benediction. A tradition. A blessing. I
have danced down concrete ramps with my sister after a
playoff win, and echoed with the voice of a dream-like,
sold-out crowd, and kept score like a vigil in the death
of a season. I have sat beside my mother as fireworks
outlined the night and headlights raced down I-70
in July. I have witnessed the slow blink of fireflies in
the backyard to the sound of the game crackling out
from the transistor radio. I have seen Monarchs fly and
Royals crowned and a city alight with blue November
joy. I have sweated as the summer slid by around me,
legs sticking to the plastic seat, Midwest air heavy with
humidity and hope, and been happy. And been alive. I
have walked through the gates at Kauffman Stadium
and been home.

What Doesn't Happen in Paris

In Paris, it rains with abandon. My sister and I seek shelter
in the Louvre's long hallways. I find a bench and make myself
a statue. Mona Lisa's face is cracked with age. I put a hand

to my cheek knowing it won't last the centuries. The rain
bleeds into Metro tunnels. Convoys of gleaming ghosts
hurtle past, rattling through pitch. At Victor Hugo station

I picture blood-stained sewers and the sorrowed weight of
revolutions lost. Water soaks my skin without regard. We
finally find a doctor up a coiled metal staircase. She tells

me it's going to be okay. Hot chocolate with a friend
makes it so. I trip along the Seine and go to ground.
My knee is red and soaked but I drag myself forward.

That night, we drink wine together and my headache
leaves me quietly. My cat is well and my mom is well and
I haven't missed home in days. The Eiffel Tower radiates

before us. I squeeze my sister's hand and close my eyes
at this reflection of my dreams. The raindrops fog around
us. I tell the city that I am not afraid.

Of the Pleiades

My friend loves what others have trouble
loving: her snakes that bite her lightly so blood
drips down her skin; plants that need a little
extra care in the cold; rats and their ribcages
collapsing down; poets who are learning to care
for themselves. She builds wings one feather
at a time and shares volcanic honey so we understand
sweetness. She is as close to magic as I know.

Her writing cradles owl flight alongside assonance;
wraps art around skeletons of data; the dead
among the living who want to understand the dead.
I watch animals take shape around her with
the intention of brush and pen. She makes waterfalls
rush and moss to comfort and knows which of her
snakes is shyest; which petals make the pinkest
jelly; what the cards have in store for us all.

One night we all followed her out into the black
beside the empty rosebushes, because she'd
learned how to weld, and to make light, and to
give what glows to the darkness. Later her two
hands held my arm and added ink to my skin as
I stared around at the love that can happen when
you lay your words as bare as a poet's heart; as
an empty shoreline; as a ruin smoothed by time
and all the weather of the years.

I think of the hard-won glow of her handiwork in the
blackness; of the light of us all in the moon.
The resolute way we breathed together, as steady
as the tide I've never glimpsed.

Succulents in Winter

I go alone in February to the nursery greenhouses;
receive my cream-colored planter and place my
hands into the soil. It's soft darkness on my hands,
under my fingernails. I pace the rows of cacti as
strained sunlight filters in. Stare hard at symmetry
and sharpened edges and silver-green succulents
waiting patiently for someone to choose them. One,
two, three, I carry with love to the wooden bench. Fit
them snugly together with more soil, more care. I layer
pebbles to keep all the gentleness in. I brush excess dirt
from my dry, cracked knuckles; gather my new plants in
close. I keep them wrapped in my arms, safe from the
coldest wind. Place them by my window, nearest sparse
and western sun. There is a kinship in wintering together.

Wringing Myths from the Rain-Steeped New Year

The rain is rising up. It grows with a
passionate quickness, as if the deluge
is the only proof of love the sky has left
for drought-struck, winter earth. Even still,
the streetlights arc down the road like
Ariadne's red thread, a beckoning home
as the storm picks up. As the news gets
worse. Lightning lines the trees. The
white-hot slashing of it reminds me that
Ariadne gifted the required sword, too.
She knew both how easy it is to lose
yourself, as well as the steadying feel
of something to cut through the darkness.
I take a deep breath, pull my hood up,
tighten the laces of my boots. I secure
myself as best I can before the plunge.
I carry too many burdens to the new year.
Outside, the water floods my boots; soaks
the once-bright yellow of my jacket; streams
into my eyes. The flashes come more quickly.
The thunder is loud enough that I give in to a
pent-up scream. Finally, an excuse to yell into
the angry, desperate, fog-stained night. My
hands shake as they work to unknot sodden,
gold-tipped laces. My breaths come too fast
and too fearful. I light lonely candles. Dream
all my worst fears before sleeping. Watch
the water flow down the hill in the aftermath

of stillness. I'm tired of labyrinth games and blind corners and monsters lurking in the shadows; in my heart. In my heart, I search for shelter. For gateways and leave-taking. For a whetstone hidden in my pocket. I sharpen what I can. The rain is rising up.

Ballad of Lightning

In college, in the middle of Kansas, I learned from glorious women. They draped buzzing August classrooms in kindness, in gravity, in the grace of all their words and truths. We knew just one part of each other, but it was a sacred, vaulted part—the part of our words upon our papers, our voices resting one atop the other. So when my professor handed us the old quote "To keep passing open windows," to carry our hope amidst all the darkness in our pens and hearts, I listened. I did not forget.

In the hospital, in the hardest August of my life, I walked past windows full of light. My neck was tight with black stitches splitting and gathering my wounded skin as I worked until the sun went down, rushed to the hospital between jobs, learned life doesn't wait for you to heal before it takes another swing. And so, alone on a still, blank hospital floor, I realized this is loving past open windows: to stitch your life together even as the thread is ripped away, to cry your agonies without reservation beneath a thousand different skies, and to stand up at the microphone anyway—no matter how hopeless; no matter how heartsick or hemorrhaging.

And if love is the ballad before the horror, love is the ballad after it—the open windows and the sun beyond them, the breeze as you lean on the sill, the words carved into your heart, the courage to keep walking and knowing the bravest thing we can do is speak our grief before the heavens. Love, I think, is the women who taught me to gather my storm.

In my dreams, I am in the bright gallery. Love fills the room from floor to rafter. At the mic, I rub pearl dust and mercy on my eyelids. I crush lightning and love on my lips.

Confessions from Tornado Alley

There is a crawling in me. I feel it every day I stagnate in
the Kansas wind working until night creeps up. There is

a writhing like cicadas tunneling from out the earth, sky-
seeking, air-dreaming, skin-thrumming, drone-screaming.

My fingers warm my wine through my borrowed glass.
The summer thunder licks at my ears as ants swarm all

this bittersweetness. I take walks in cemeteries to revel
in my quiet living. Sometimes my chest squeezes tight,

like my fist closing around cloudy water. So much I seek
is peace. So much, absolution. I count the days of truest

happiness on one hand every year. Each moment, I
think a little more of longing. Of how I walked into the

desert and saw a cactus blooming, and I thought, *too
much sunshine; too much light.* If I stay here any longer it

will swallow me up. A year ago I saw NEOWISE hang
hazy in the Missouri sky and nothing changed in me.

I stare out at the lake and see so much that drowns. A
crash of tiredness settles on my shoulders. I ask nature

to absolve me. I ask poetry to absolve me. I ask aching
feet and church-bright candles and dead irises to

absolve me. In the cavern I walk and walk until the
light can't reach. Sometimes the chasm's so deep,

the pit goes on forever. My breaths are elegy.
My eyes, the blood and the burn.

So I Wouldn't Be Alone

January smells like rain in spring. The year is
new. The days are broken things. Last week
my friend came over so I wouldn't be alone.
I opened the door to a kindness that scared
me with its softened edges. I roll the window
down in the plummeting air. Cry until my body
aches with it; get lost in my own city. In the night
I wake to blood between my teeth. Just another
hurt to breathe through. I listen as Mary Oliver's
geese lose themselves to the darkening sky. I ask
them not to go. I am tired of losing what is good
and precious in the world. I clutch my pen tightly;
remember, in college, writing, *you are never as
alone as you think*. Remember breathing that
poetry into the garden air. I am trying to have
courage as the sun goes down.

Soliloquy for My Eighteen-Year-Old Self

I hear the leaves blowing in the trees,
shhhing and soothing like a parent to
the child they gather close against any
horror. Some still are darkest green even
as the cold crests, a violent storm surge,
ragged clouds and chilling rains and a
swelling moon carried in by the frothing
current. Sirens send their clarion call curling
through the air, emergency after emergency
after emergency. This is America. You can
imagine what the emergencies are. The L
battles back and forth into the dark, in and
out of my hearing, quicker and more urgent
than the inconsolable clamor of my heart.
Some days my home might as well be here.
In the city's cemeteries, the dead lie beneath
sunset-colored leaves. They cannot see the
stone writing that has rubbed away; the
tombstones cracked in two; blood-colored
leaves we crush beneath our boots as we
weave between too many graves to count.
The window crack lets in autumn's breath
with an ominous hint of winter. One sister
sleeps in the next room. One sleeps in
Colorado, waiting for the snow, pieces of
this city creeping like frost across her open
heart. The last sister sits awake—half in
shadow, half in the lukewarm wash of Chicago
streetlights and jack-o-lantern glow. Find me

when the sun sets earlier than ever. Find me
as the temperature plummets and grave ground
grows cold and quiet. When the November
rain starts, find me. Tomorrow the starlit train
will carry me away.

Nocturne for the Baseball Streets

No field of dreams in Bleeding Kansas. Just highways
crisscrossing state lines and two cities on two rivers and
Missouri blinking in the night holding half my youth

to my grandpa's sodbuster chest. No field of dreams, true,
but still the stadium stands like a landlocked lighthouse, a
place of worship, a refugium after a fire, still the people

line up with their blue-gold shirts, their daughters and
sisters, their World Series hopes and October dreams,
because now the gates are open and the people are

back and the joy stretches from foul pole to foul pole.
Baseball breathes and we all breathe with it, gulp the
summer air into lungs that have held our breath for it;

starved for it; prayed for it. Fountains sing sing sing in the
outfield as I climb the concrete steps to my cheap-seat
throne because the left-field line is my home, too. And

when the fireworks burst above our settled bodies, it's my
mom in the dark beside me. My mom taught me baseball
love like her father wrapped around her—his family glory

in baseball fields, a Palcher on every base in heartland dirt
or Europe's dust. They grinned when they slid home and
their brother was above them to pull them up like they

learned on Strawberry Hill, the city outlined at their
backs. Baseballs have always soared over the city;
Monarchs flying 'round the base paths; Brooklyn Avenue

ringing with the downtown crowds as Satchel, Buck, and
Jackie aimed for the stratosphere. See, baseball was their
language, their fight, the heartbeat in their chests and the

jubilation in their stride, and the streets were lit with it,
the city alive with it, the men crowned with it. Trace I-70
out of the proud, strong past to where we cheer from the

top of Kauffman. Mr. And Mrs. K wave in the outfield
and my mom is in the dark beside me. When we slide
home and someone's reaching out, we feel unshakable
baseball love, and the stadium lights never stop shining.

Listening to "Stardust" by Artie Shaw
& His Orchestra

The last time I visited my grandpa's house, it
was nearly empty. Bed frames and mattresses
leaned against pastel pinks of floral wallpaper.
The hallway was clear of decades of memories,
void of black and white, void even of color. No
more Army uniform behind the office doors,
dog tags long tucked away. No more Colorado
placemats he used to carefully set out every time
we came over. The gifted golden clock that spun
around while we spoke was gone—and that mounted
piece of the Berlin Wall, and the aging wooden
croquet set, and the yellow, fringed patio umbrella,
and the Colmar magnet we bought him last year in
France. We carried it across the ocean for him.
The last things I saw: peeling train stickers at his
computer desk where he composed North Carolina
emails and kept track of his Hearts scores every day.
The flowers my father planted carefully in the front
yard. The bushes growing tall and wild near the steps
where he waved goodbye, shouting *auf wiedersiehn*
from the porch. The bathroom lightbulbs he gleefully
told us would last for twenty years, at least. The wrought
iron storm door, heavy and still. The backyard gate dully
gleaming in the afternoon light. The sycamore twice as
tall as the house, sun winking between the leaves. I took
a few lonely CDs with me, carefully labelled with permanent
marker. Slid one disc into my car that night. Smiled as
Artie Shaw's orchestra blared from my speakers on the
dark drive home. It sounded so much like getting older.

love notes and dissent

after Langston Hughes and Emma Lazarus

no time for grief; not anymore. a
neighbor needs you. a sister needs
you. a stranger needs you. so wear
your mask proudly. read langston
loudly, let america be truth to
devastation. let it be love notes
to each other. let love notes be
black ink on ballots and lace-
collared dissent. let dissent be
the hands we hold out to each
other. let our hands be the
bridges we're building. let our
bridges cross miles, oceans,
origins. let our origins be everywhere
someone is dreaming. let our dreams
be without cages, without tear gas,
without walls. let our walls be a
memory. let our memories be
unflinching. let our unflinching
hearts crack, but let them crack open.
let our open arms lock together and
embrace the yearning to breathe
free. let our freedom be our
responsibility, our responsibility
our outrage, our outrage
our hope. let our hope be a
promise to do better than our
histories. let the histories we write

be something we're proud of
tomorrow. let tomorrow be the time
we stand though we're shaking. let
our stand be remembered as a
transmutation of grief; as the future
we forge from these ashes and nights.
and let our nights lead to brilliant,
incandescent dawns—grateful sunrises.
we exist side-by-side, reading poetry to
november air, pledging ourselves to each
other in that fragile valor called faith

golden shovel: election season

after "love notes and dissent"

in my poetry workshop, our professor used to bring us
    clementines. we
unraveled the rough skin as we spoke in stanzaic love,
    let our trust exist
outside our bodies for a while. poems still taste like
    tangy citrus, a side

of little bites of elegy. couplets still hang like honey in
    the air. in july by
the wetland rushes, i saw a crane take flight. its wings
    beating wide side-
to-side were better than a crown of sonnets on my
    head. a year of reading

mary oliver conjured devotions amongst the water lilies;
    crafted poetry
in the snake's quick slither and the skunk's rustle off the
    paths. i want to
live in the love of those metaphors forever. there once
    was a november

where i prayed in ross gay's gratitude. i shouted
    tenderness to the air.
i want the choice that's harder. all around me are brave
    people, pledging
courage in the night. one hopeless winter we took an
    evening for ourselves.

we read steely words of revolutionaries come before us.
    we wanted to
carry fear and hope together. i read hélène berr to the
    crowd. with each
lifted voice we beat back the darkness. i run poems one
    after the other

through the chaos of my mind. whisper Brooks' "Paul
    Robeson" in
invocation of some peace. promises mean something in
    poems that
we write, recite, carry close against our stuttering hearts.
    it's fragile—

to love and write amidst the hatred flooding up on every
    side. valor
is tough to come by. so remember that hopeless winter.
    how we called
each other to light. we spoke love in our poetry. we
    spread quiet faith.

the year of blessings and tenderness

after Ross Gay

revelations fall on a body much
like snow does, much like leaves
give everything up to trust
in wind and open air. the year
reeks of hospitals and uncertainty,
of the kind of fear you pray will
never find you. i hold my mother's
hand more than i used to. i try to
fold my heart into each touch,
into every whorled fingerprint.

and i am thankful even in this
longest night for april afternoons—
for tulips glorious in sunlight, and
laughing on creaky merry-go-
rounds, and to be together and
bright-eyed and alive for however
long we're given.

i know fragility. i know it in the heavy wait
for ct results and the breaths doctors make
you hold; in slow-healing incisions, skin
knitting back together; in every moment
we stand shakily and wonder how our
cells might be growing dying twisting
within us.

these months i have thrown my head
back and bared my life unto the world—
to the doctors' probing hands and the
scalpel's metal bite and a million eyes
that ripped into the scar dragging
across my neck.

i've closed my eyes to hands around
my throat, to the radioactive decay
within my veins, to the stillness of
medical imaging and the exposure
of a hospital gown. contrast burned
inside me.

there are so many pieces of my body
that exist without permission—just
farewelled youth and diagnoses. if
i had any advantage as i sat defenseless,
neck outstretched, it was that the year
had already cut me open

so i pray in bathroom stalls; on
subway trains; to the lightning-carved
up sky—*God*, i whisper, fingers drifting
to the fine pink line beneath my chin—
grant me tenderness in this hour of the
hardest choices; for my neck, scarred
and soft, stripped clean before the new
year. let me face the coming of the light;
the days growing warmer; the crocuses
reaching—

they are aglow like my
mother's voice from the next room.
she is harmonied with the transistor
radio. here is my pulse; my life
for the taking

Ten Ways I Know I'm Alive

1. The leaves beneath my feet crunch-snap as I walk.
Early October and yellows are just beginning to manifest.
Sometimes I smile to myself in the middle of realizing
I'm happier. The air is turning and the light is leaving.
My mother, saying, *kickin' leaves*; my father, walking;
picking out the brightest colors fallen to bring her.

2. England–stone and pasture and hills and stillest water–
surrounds us. We dance a ceilidh at my cousin's wedding.
We dance with people we've never met from countries
we've never been to until our faces are joy-flushed and the
barn is steeped in sweat and laughter. *I'm pouring more water
than pints*, the bartender says, chagrined. My hand in some-
one's hand. My dress eddying around my body. My feet,
stamping; the fiddle, soaring; my love, thundering.

3. This world is abloom. Spring returned in triumph; in
trust. One by one I gather pink petals in my palm. I hold
them steady for a moment–then I give them to the sky.
They land on my shoulders; in my brown-grey hair. *You
are here*, like the sculpture garden heart with the river
winding 'round it. I spy LOVE on the wall. It's in the
foundation. Above us, it's blossoms. Blossoms forever.

4. We sit on the rooftop, the fire chasing the chill from
our fingertips. Last night in the city–for now. The Red
Line rattles by insistently. My phone quietly glows, its
speakers offering up Sara Bareilles songs to the Chicago
night. *Sing along*, I say, and I feel the music in the red brick

of the building and the hot chocolate warm between my hands. Skyscrapers blink steady in the distance. I could dream here.

5. My friend and I let our feet sink into sand. We have never been here. The years fall down between us as the sun sets over sanguine mountains. Sand dunes flow like waves, like softest silk. A thousand footprints will be gone tomorrow morning. *Remember,* we say in the car on the way back. My sister drives by moonlight. The car is full of story.

6. When the fog rolls out, the stars come out. Ninety-six floors of perspective on the year–on all the wounds; the stitches; the scars. My glass is full of light as the horizon darkens. I read by candle flickers as the city unfurls beneath me. Whisper *thank you.* It's the first time I've breathed all year. I don't know anything of the coming darknesses. But in that moment, the light is enough.

7. I take off work one April afternoon. My sister is in town. We meet for lunch–three sisters; three sets of dreams. We stride up and down the streets before we have to part, searching for hundreds of heart statues adorning the city. *You have to pose*, we tell her. So we throw our arms out. Now, all. Now, together.

8. My head is detonations of agony but I have hours of road to go. Wear sunglasses to dim the world down. Strangle the steering wheel as rain starts; as night falls; as my skull shivers apart. Sometimes I'm alone on the highway. The musical I attended earlier echoes through my head: *Orpheus. Eurydice. A long journey through the dark.* I beat down memories of a different highway. A different rain. I will myself home again.

9. The museum gallery pulses, three thousand bulbs
blinking in synchronous rhythm. I reach out my hand.
It's bathed in luminescence. I cradle radiance. Electricity
sparks above me; spreads from my epicenter. At the same
time, a sound: my heart, beating. *Thump, thump. Thump,
thump. Thump, thump.* My heart, for the whole room to
hear and see; my life to witness. What wonder can spread
from us. What tenderness.

10. My brother and sister-in-law make soup on the first
day that feels like fall. We gather ourselves in the glow
of the kitchen as the rain seeps down the windows. My
nephews grin. One cools his soup with little exhales.
Together we set ourselves against the sorrows. My sister-
in-law cuts grilled cheeses like our mom does, says, *I
thought we needed this.* She's right, I realize, as I head
out into the fog and damp. This is what we need.

Notes

Little Women (1870), by Louisa May Alcott, is available to the public through the Library of Congress.

"Wayfarer Memory" references Nelson Algren's *Chicago: City on the Make.*

"roots and coffins" references Walt Whitman's "Song of Myself."

"i call the mountain mother" references Robert Frost's "Birches."

"where the strawberries grew" references the Kansas City, Kansas, immigrant memorial.

"Landlocked," "Twelve Days Pass Between the Death and the Funeral," "We're Here Because," and "So I Wouldn't Be Alone" are after Neil Hilborn's poems, "Our Numbered Days."

"November 11, 2016: Poyntz Avenue" references Leonard Cohen's song, "Hallelujah."

"A Day in Giverny" references the former Nelson Atkins Museum of Art exhibit "Monet's *Water Lilies: From Dawn to Dusk.*"

"What Comes Back" is referencing the photograph *Couple in the Tuileries Garden, Paris, 1945* by LAPI Roger-Viollet.

"Outside Carl Sandburg's House" references Carl Sandburg's "Chicago" and Nelson Algren's *Chicago: City on the Make.*

"I Leave Monet's *Water Lilies* at Every Shooting"
references Bernie Boston's 1967 photo, *Flower Power*.

"Stage Magic" references *King Lear* and *Romeo and Juliet*,
both by William Shakespeare.

"An Hour at Orsay Station" references *Starry Night Over
the Rhône* by Vincent van Gogh.

"By Memory" is after "Summer Haibun" by Aimee
Nezhukumatathil and "What I Would Like to Grow in
My Garden" by Katherine Riegel.

"We're Here Because" is after Edward
Dwyer, "Auld Lang Syne," and John Green.

"Ballad of Lightning" references *The Hotel New Hampshire*
by John Irving, and the Queen song, "Keep Passing
Open Windows."

"So I Wouldn't Be Alone" references "Wild Geese" by
Mary Oliver.

"love notes and dissent" references "Let America Be
America Again" by Langston Hughes and "The New
Colossus" by Emma Lazarus.

"the year of blessings and tenderness" is after Ross Gay's
"Bringing the Shovel Down" and "Again."

"Ten Ways I Know I'm Alive": Parts 3 and 6 reference
the 2022 Parade of Hearts in Kansas City, and art by

Jeremy Collins. Part 4 references "Once Upon Another Time" by Sara Bareilles. Part 8 references "Wait for Me" by Anaïs Mitchell. Part 9 references former Kemper Museum of Contemporary Art exhibit *Pulse Topology* by Rafael Lozano-Hemmer.

Catherine Strayhall grew up in Kansas and earned her bachelor's degree at Kansas State University, where she was a two-time winner of the Sullivan Poetry Award. Her work has appeared in *KANSAS!* magazine, the *Johnson County Arts & Heritage Center*, and the *Kansas City Star*. She has been featured several times in the online publication *Poets Reading the News*, going on to serve as an associate editor. Catherine lives in the Kansas City area, where she's been working in libraries and education. Outside of work, she enjoys attending sporting events, fan conventions, and the theater. *Dress Me Like a Prizefighter* is her first full-length collection.

This project was made possible, in part, by generous support from the Osage Arts Community.

Osage Arts Community provides temporary time, space and support for the creation of new artistic works in a retreat format, serving creative people of all kinds — visual artists, composers, poets, fiction and nonfiction writers. Located on a 152-acre farm in an isolated rural mountainside setting in Central Missouri and bordered by ¾ of a mile of the Gasconade River, OAC provides residencies to those working alone, as well as welcoming collaborative teams, offering living space and workspace in a country environment to emerging and mid-career artists. For more information, visit us at www.osageac.org

Osage Arts Community

www.ingramcontent.com/pod-product-compliance
Lightning Source LLC
Chambersburg PA
CBHW030915140626
46545CB00017B/2357